Fourth Dimensional Spirituality School

INSTITUTE FOR CHURCH GROWTH

Fourth Dimensional Spirituality School

INSTITUTE FOR CHURCH GROWTH

*Companion Workbook to the
Fourth Dimension Spirituality Books*

by Dr. David Yonggi Cho

Bridge-Logos
Alachua, Florida 32615

Bridge-Logos

Alachua, Florida 32615

Fourth Dimensional Spirituality School
by Dr. David Yonggi Cho
Institute for Church Growth, Seoul, South Korea

Printed in the United States of America.

Library of Congress Catalog Card Number: 2008923865
Internationsl Standard Book Number: 978-088270-482-1

CONTENTS

Lesson	Lesson Title	Page
Lesson 1:	The Meaning and Significance of Fourth Dimensional Spirituality	1
Lesson 2:	Fourth Dimensional Spirituality: Thinking (Theory)	7
Lesson 3:	Fourth Dimensional Spirituality: Thinking (Application)	13
Lesson 4:	Fourth Dimensional Spirituality: Faith (Theory)	19
Lesson 5:	Fourth Dimensional Spirituality: Faith (Application)	25
Lesson 6:	Fourth Dimensional Spirituality: Dreams (Theory)	33
Lesson 7:	Fourth Dimensional Spirituality: Dreams (Application)	41
Lesson 8:	Fourth Dimensional Spirituality: Words (Theory)	47
Lesson 9:	Fourth Dimensional Spirituality: Words (Application)	53
Lesson 10:	Developing Fourth Dimensional Spirituality: Prayer Discipline	59
Lesson 11:	Developing Fourth Dimensional Spirituality: Word Discipline	65
Lesson 12:	Developing Fourth Dimensional Spirituality: The Holy Spirit Discipline	71
Answers:	Fourth Dimension Sprituality Answers to the Study Questions	77

The Meaning and the Significance

OF FOURTH DIMENSIONAL SPIRITUALITY

One Iraqi man had dropped by the office of a Theology professor in America. This man suffered greatly, as one of his legs was partially amputated due to a train accident. The Iraqi was accompanied by friends; some friends of the professor were also there. The professor prayed for the Iraqi in his office. Laying his hands on the Iraqi, the professor shouted, "In the name of Jesus of Nazareth, may the legs be extended. In the name of Jesus of Nazareth, may the legs be extended! "

The professor repeatedly shouted for over five minutes until he was drenched in sweat, however, nothing happened to the Iraqi's legs. Everyone present also prayed, in hopes that the man in need of healing might not be disappointed. Never losing hope, the professor stretched his arms toward the Iraqi and asked him to confess, "God is living. Jesus the Son of God is my Savior., and He will heal me."

Then the professor came closer and said, "In the name of Jesus of Nazareth, may the legs be extended! In the name of Jesus of Nazareth, may the legs be extended!"

At that exact moment, something unbelievable happened: In less than thirty seconds, the Iraqi man's legs were extended. Everyone around marveled at God's power and praised God. The crippled Iraqi could stand firm. He accepted Jesus, who had just healed him, as his Savior. This is a true story. Miracles aren't the only elements of a Christian life,nevertheless, God uses them according to His will for very serious missions. Have you ever experienced miracles? If so, share the stories with each other.

Search for Information

How Do the First, Second, Third, and Fourth Dimensions Differ?

I might have understood the distinctions between these dimensions well when I first learned them in high school, but they now seem vague. You may not realize just how helpful it is in the Christian life to know the difference. Let's find out.

First Dimension

The First Dimension is a realm possibly expressed by a *single* factor. A simple *line* is a good example. A *line* is initially determined by a single spot. The elements existing in the First Dimension consist of a segment, line, and half a line. Length is the only quantifiable measure. There is no height or width in the First Dimension.

Second Dimension

We need two dimensions to quantify the Second Dimension. *Area* is the best example. *Area* is a measure which involves width and length. Existing examples in the Second Dimension are triangles, rectangles, and various types of polygonal shapes.

Third Dimension

The Third Dimension has three dimensions to define its shape. It is a concept best defined by *volume.* Volume utilizes height in addition to length and width. The real world we live in is three-dimensional.

Fourth Dimension

A single dot has zero dimensions. When the spot is on a line, it separates the line into the right and left part. If an endless line is drawn on a plane, a line (the First Dimension) separates the area (the Second Dimension) into the right and the left spheres. Again, if we assume there is an infinite space, it can be a departing section of the infinite cubic (the Third Dimension). It is important to indicate that the dimension which separates the other dimensions always has one less dimension. We can conclude that the Third Dimension we currently live in is an ending section, which separates us from the immense Fourth Dimension.

From the point of view that the Second Dimension contains the First Dimension and the Third Dimension contains the Second, we can also conclude that the Fourth Dimension contains the Third Dimension. Thus, the spiritual world of the Fourth Dimension controls that of the Third Dimension.

Encounter with the Bible

Please Read Hebrews 11:1-6:

Now faith is being sure of what we hope for and certain of what we do not see. This is what the ancients were commended for. By faith we understand that the universe was formed at God's command, so that what is seen was not made out of what was visible. By faith Abel offered God a better sacrifice than Cain did. By faith he was commended as a righteous man, when God spoke well of his offerings. And by faith he still speaks, even though he is dead. By faith Enoch was taken from this life, so that he did not experience death; he could not be found, because God had taken him away. For before he was taken, he was commended as one who pleased God. And without faith it is impossible to please God, because anyone who comes to him must believe that he exists and that he rewards those who earnestly seek him.

1. The text is called "the Faith lesson" and it introduces the nature and the substance of faith. How does the text define faith? (v.1)

2. By faith we understand that the universe was formed by God's commandments. What is the origin of the visible things in the world? (v.3)

    _____

    _____

    _____

3. How could Abel and Enoch be commended by God?

    _____

    _____

    _____

4. What are the two things those who come to God must believe?
    1. _____
    2. _____

5. How do you explain to unbelievers that *what is seen was made from the invisible?* Practice it with your fellow students.

   The Christian faith is one which people believe in God almighty. It is not a lifeless religion full of rigid dogmas. Its power lies in the daily application of God's Word and of the living God, who still works in us (Romans 4:17).

1. Fourth Dimensional God

   God is over all and in all (Ephesians 4:6). God is in the world, but at the same time, He is over all and above all. Being invisible, He brings all invisible things together and controls them. It was when God created the world that He clearly showed His lordship.
In the beginning, when the earth was formless and empty and the Spirit of God was hovering over the waters, creation occurred (Genesis 1:2). When the Spirit, which is Fourth Dimensional, worked in the Third Dimensional world, the new world such as light, expansion, earth, and so on came into being.

❖ Share with one another, any incident or experience in your life which made you realize that God reigns over the world.

2. The Elements of Fourth Dimensional Spirituality

The Fourth Dimensional Spirituality is about training these four elements: thought, faith, dreams, and words. These elements control the Fourth Dimensional world. The channel through which our Fourth Dimensional God works in our Third Dimensional world is through these very elements: thought, faith, dreams, and words.

A. Thinking (Proverbs 23:7)

Thinking is never defined by time and space, but it controls all things. A change in a man's thought life is immediately reflected on the Third Dimension. For example, when a negative thought about others comes to a person's mind, it first brings ruin upon himself. But he who is geared with positive thinking shows its good effects physically, through his personal and professional life.

❖ Share your experience, if you have any, of how a small tiny change in thinking produced huge outcomes.

B. Faith (Matthew 17:20)

Faith is a huge power that can change the Third Dimensional world through the Fourth Dimensional one. Jesus said, "According to your faith will it be done to you" (Matthew 9:29), "If you can? Everything is possible for him who believes" (Mark 9:23). Faith produces miracles.

❖ Share your experiences with one another, about how your faith has miraculously turned circumstances around and gotten you through a crisis.

C. Dreams (Proverbs 29:18)

Many times, we have observed how a dream has changed the world. A dream from God, and not merely from unconscious ambition, is much more powerful. One who is given a vision from God through the Holy Spirit can change the whole world.

❖ Share any stories you may have heard, about someone who once endured hardship and later experienced success by holding onto a vision.

D. Words (Proverbs 6:2)

A word is a special quality only men possess. A word, spoken by a man created in God's image, has tremendous authority. When words are spoken, *it will be so.* Success or failure depends on what kinds of words one uses.

❖ Share experiences with one another, where something happened exactly according to what you had said.

3. Fourth Dimensional Spirituality Transforms Human Life

When God created man, he breathed the breath of life into his nostrils. And the man became a living being (Genesis 2:7). God continued the momentum of the Fourth Dimensional spiritual world through man. Because man is a spiritual being, he is connected with the Fourth Dimension even though he lives in the Third Dimensional world.

The human spirit controls the flesh, which is Third Dimensional. When man's spirit hurts, his body becomes sick; and when his spirit is lively, his body becomes healthy.

The reason why the Fourth Dimension is so important is because it has power to change the Third Dimension – the real world. But the visible Third Dimensional world can only be changed after the Fourth Dimensional world has changed.

Application and Practice

■ In this workbook we have studied the meaning and the significance of Fourth Dimensional Spirituality. Share anything new you may have learned.

■ Share with each other, your resolution in starting the Fourth Dimensional Spirituality school and also your specific goals you would like to achieve.

■ Share with each other, your weakest of the four elements in Fourth Dimensional Spirituality. Dedicate a time of prayer to ensure a life full of God's power (three minutes).

Key Bible Words

What is seen was not made out of what was visible (Hebrews 11:3).

Quote

"Fill your thinking, mind and action with God's Fourth Dimension. And you will enjoy a new life like never experienced before."

—Dr. David Yonggi Cho

Homework

Write a testimony about experiencing Fourth Dimensional Spirituality in your life.

_____

_____

_____

_____

Bibliography

The Fourth Dimensional Spirituality (Institute for Church Growth) by Dr. David Yonggi Cho

~Notes~

2

LESSON

Fourth Dimensional Spirituality: Thinking

THEORY

Somebody conducted an experiment. He secretly removed caffeine from coffee and served it to ten people who had difficulty falling sleeping after drinking coffee. But the results showed that even upon drinking decaffeinated coffee, the subjects still could not sleep. He then placed caffeine into milk and served it to them. This time, they fell asleep soundly.

Why did this happen? The research team came to the conclusion that the problem was mind over matter. They could not sleep because their negative mind had conditioned them to believe that drinking coffee would keep them alert.

In conclusion, it was their negative minds — not caffeine — that kept them from sleeping. Though they later drank caffeine, they were still able to get good sleep because they believed they were drinking milk instead.

❖ Have you ever experienced anything similar to this? If so, share your experiences with each other.

Check List for Self-assessment of Fourth Dimensional Thinking

Although the following list may not be the absolute in standards for Fourth Dimensional thinking, this list will help you closely align yourself to Fourth Dimensional Spirituality with regard to your thinking, beliefs, dreams, and words.

Five points represents the "highest" and one point represents "the lowest" to each question. Circle your answer below:

1. I start my day by meditating on God.

  1   2   3   4   5

2. I try to think positively rather than negatively.

  1   2   3   4   5

7

3. I am slow to anger and more apt to tolerate someone when they make mistakes.

         1   2   3   4   5

4. I pray for myself when I sense there are negative factors in my thinking (worry, anger, inferiority complex, etc.)

         1   2   3   4   5

5. I am thankful I'm saved and blessed.

         1   2   3   4   5

6. I do not allow unhealthy and negative thinking to dwell in my mind. Instead of wallowing in them, I reject them.

         1   2   3   4   5

7. I feel like my mind is controlled by the joy of the Holy Spirit.

         1   2   3   4   5

8. Whenever I think of God, I can feel him as a Father who is kind and cares for me.

         1   2   3   4   5

9. I always try to memorize Scriptures to help me think biblically.

         1   2   3   4   5

10. I have a clear image of the work accomplished before I start the goal.

         1   2   3   4   5

Write your total number of points here: My points: (_____)

Results

Over 40 points:
You are full of the Fourth Dimensional thinking.
Move on with your work until you reach your peak.

30-40 points:
You are average in your Fourth Dimensional thinking.
It's time to make an effort for your progress.

Below 30 points:
You have opportunities for more Fourth Dimensional thinking.
Discipline yourself to see with God's perspective, whenever the chance presents itself.

❖ Check your points and present your scores to each other.

Encounter with the Bible

Read Romans 8:5-9:

Those who live according to the sinful nature have their minds set on what that nature desires; but those who live in accordance with the Spirit have their minds set on what the Spirit desires. The mind of sinful man is death, but the mind controlled by the Spirit is life and peace; the sinful mind is hostile to God. It does not submit to God's law, nor can it do so. Those controlled by the sinful nature cannot please God. You, however, are controlled not by the sinful nature but by the Spirit, if the Spirit of God lives in you. And if anyone does not have the Spirit of Christ, he does not belong to Christ.

1.   The text says the new law of the Spirit earned in Christ Jesus set the Christians free from the law of sin and death. The passage also mentions the difference between the one who lives according to the sinful nature and the one who lives in accordance with the Spirit.

❖ What do those who live according to the sinful nature and those who live in accordance with the Spirit set their minds on? (v.5)

2. What is the difference between the mind of a sinful man and the mind controlled by the Spirit? (v.6)

_____

_____

3. Why is the man controlled by the sinful nature unable to please God? (v.7)

_____

_____

4. What does the Apostle Paul say is *proof that we are Christians?* (v.9)

_____

_____

5. Through the text, we realize that the difference in thought may decide life or death. Do you have your mind set on what the nature desires, or on what the Spirit desires?

_____

_____

Thinking has a great influence on our lives. The main difference between someone who succeeds and someone who doesn't isn't necessarily determined by opportunity, background, education, luck, or even smarts. It is the difference in their thinking.

The Significance of Thinking

1. Thinking has an influence on health.

Someone who believes he is happy, although he is sick, lives longer than the one who is healthy but is not happy. This shows that even health is controlled by our thinking.

Illustration 1:

A study, conducted by the medical Hospital in Maryland University, studied elders over the age of sixty-five for ten years. It showed that those who maintained happiness, even through illness, lived longer by more than five years than those who were healthy but were unhappy.

2. Thinking has an influence on physical activity.

To think pleasantly helps produce endorphins which prevents aging and improves memory. On the other hand, unpleasant thinking stimulates the brain to produce adrenocortical hormones which causes high blood pressure, heart disease, and osteoporosis.

Illustration 2:

In his book *A Great Revolution in the Brain World,* Haruyama Shiegeo insists that only pleasant emotions can produce the brain endorphins which prevent aging and improves memory. But unpleasant emotions are widely known among scientists to stimulate production of the adrenocortical hormone, which causes high blood pressure, heart disease, osteoporosis, and mental disease.

3. Thinking has an influence on human relationships.

An old Korean proverb says, "One good word repays a million dollars in debt." Research indicates that if a man speaks five million words throughout his entire life, according to the proverb, the man has the potential to pay off infinite debt throughout his lifetime. As an ore turns out to be a precious gem after tempering it, our words can become the art of creating shining gems if we refine them.

A kind word opens one's heart, while an unfriendly word can hurt or ruin a good relationship. Words which contain criticism, blame, and complaints worsen relationships among people, while productive words create good vibes even under bad conditions.

4. Thinking has an influence on environment.

Tomorrow's success depends on how one thinks today. If your thinking is bound in your circumstances, its potential is also limited. But if you keep expanding your thinking, you can enjoy progress beyond measure.

Illustration 3:

Hitler was not fond of a couple of demographic groups: Jews and women. As a result, he was responsible for the homicide of six million Jews. And though he was often in the company of women, he never married.

His hate could perhaps be traced back to childhood. His father, a merchant, left on business travel for two or three months at a time. His mother, who probably endured much loneliness, eventually had an affair with a rich Jewish neighbor.

The young impressionable Hitler earnestly asked his mother to come back but it was to no avail. Since that time, Hitler projected his hate toward all women and Jews. One woman's sin was enough to create the murderous heart in Hitler. Many suffered as a result.

5. Thinking changes and transforms the course of life.

A single thought is a starting point for changing the purpose and direction of our lives. We will be a negative person when we think negatively and inversely, and a positive person when we think happy and positively.

Application and Practice

■ We have studied the Fourth Dimensional Spirituality: Thinking (Theory).
Have you gained new understanding? Consider the significance of thought and expand upon why it is so important.

_____

_____

■ Share your individual situation with one another. If there are reasons why you can't accept yourself as you are, explain why.

■ Dedicate a time of prayer, so that you can be a Christian who thinks in creative and positive ways, adopting a mind like God's (three minutes).

Key Bible Words

The mind of sinful man is death, but the mind controlled by the Spirit is life and peace (Romans 8:6).

Quote

"All that is thinkable is possible to realize." (Einstein)

Homework

Write down how your life is transformed when you think positively instead of negatively.

_____

_____

Bibliography

The Power of Positive Thinking by Norman Vincent Peale

~Notes~

3

LESSON

Fourth Dimensional Spirituality: Thinking

APPLICATION

Mr. Chung Moon Shik, the CEO of Jireh Electronics, started his business determined to observe the Lord's Day and to better devote himself as a Sunday school teacher.

After he quit his job that required him to work on Sunday, he started a small business. Bereaved of his father at the age of ten, he studied as a working student and graduated from night school. With only a few dollars remaining from three years of work, he started his business in the 160 square-foot, underground garage. It became so tough for him to run the business that he once thought death would be a better alternative.

In utter despair one day, he heard the message of Yonggi Cho, "Do not be misled by anything false and fruitless. Don't focus on the environment. Move on, trusting God with absolute positive faith." Being encouraged by this message, he overcame the tough situation. This key made it possible for him to overcome failure, despair, and anguish. This was the spiritual nourishment he needed and had appropriately taken.

He listened to God's Word, meditated on the Scriptures, and faithfully followed God. As a result, he became one of the best known Korean CEOs in the small business sector, with 100 million dollars in sales. The secret of his success was to think and live according to the Word of God; not his own thinking.

❖ *Have you ever experienced a complete change in your life by adopting God's thoughts as your own?*

_____

_____

_____

_____

_____

_____

Keep a Fourth Dimensional Spiritual Self-Image of Yourself

God wants us grow spiritually and physically in our personal lives, in our family lives and in our church lives. Those who are able to grow, have a clear self-image. A Christian embodies a new creature, whose status, purpose, and strengths are transformed: his status is he is a child of God; his purpose is *to be like Jesus*; his strengths are the gifts and fruits of the Holy Spirit. So, what exactly is the Fourth Dimensional self-image?

We Can Explain It Using the Acronym G R O W T H

G The first Fourth Dimensional *self-image* is GOODNESS:
He who has Fourth Dimensional Spirituality in him possesses the image of God. God is good, truthful, and holy. Someone who looks like God is kind to his parents, to his children, to his brothers, to his friends, and to his neighbors. He is a good Christian, who is holy and separated from the world.

R The second Fourth Dimensional *self-image* is REVIVAL:
Someone with Fourth Dimensional Spirituality won't merely stay within the church, but will reach beyond that. He makes an effort for renewal inwardly and revival outwardly.

O The third Fourth Dimensional *self-image* is OBEDIENCE.
He who has Fourth Dimensional Spirituality obeys the spiritual authority. A habit is soon formed, which can be seen in their daily life, to obey each other.

W The Fourth Dimensional *self-image* is WORDS.
He who has Fourth Dimensional Spirituality is ravenous about knowing the Word of God. He acquires sufficient knowledge of God, of who God is and what He does.

T The fifth Fourth Dimensional *self-image* is THANKSGIVING.
Whoever has Fourth Dimensional Spirituality knows to give thanks in all circumstances. The words "think" and "thank" have the same origin. If you think deeply, you will give thanks in all circumstances.

H The sixth Fourth Dimensional *self-image* is HUMILITY.
He who has Fourth Dimensional Spirituality is humble before God and men. He expands his enthusiasm for God into his true love for his neighbor.

Encounter with the Bible

Read Philippians 4:4-9:

Rejoice in the Lord always. I will say it again: Rejoice! Let your gentleness be evident to all. The Lord is near. Do not be anxious about anything, but in everything, by prayer and petition, with thanksgiving, present your requests to God. And the peace of God, which transcends all understanding, will guard your hearts and your minds in Christ Jesus. Finally, brothers, whatever is true, whatever is noble, whatever is right, whatever is pure, whatever is lovely, whatever is admirable—if anything is excellent or praiseworthy—think about such things. Whatever you have learned or received or heard from me, or seen in me—put it into practice. And the God of peace will be with you.

1. The text admonishes the saints of the church in Philippi regarding joy, fellowship, and supplication, which are essential to the Christian life. What is necessary for Christians to think joyfully? (v.4)

_____

_____

2. What kind of strength is required of Christians to stop negative thinking, containing or producing worry and anxiety? (v.6)

_____

_____

3. What will guard the hearts of Christians who arm themselves with prayer and supplication? (v.7)

_____

_____

_____

4. What kind of attitude is exceptionally important for believers to maintain in the Last Days? (v.8)

_____

_____

5. If anyone of you has experienced God's peace guarding your hearts and minds, share this with one another.

Our minds are like a computers; reacting according to what we have been programmed. Created in God's image, we are programmed to live a wholesome life. We should think in harmony with that.

Transformation of Thinking

You can never over emphasize the importance of a change in thinking. Thoughts are difficult to change, and they are not changed by themselves. However, the process is worth investigating.

Transformation of thinking can bring forth benefits.

Change in thinking equals change of behavior, change of habit, change of character, and change of fate. The motive behind the transformation of our thinking is Jesus Christ. We can understand God's heart through the death and resurrection of Jesus Christ. Romans 8:39 says, "Though I'm useless, I can change my heart to be filled with God's love through Jesus Christ, who loved me enough to die for me."

We have examined how the process of transforming our thinking leads to the transformation of life. Which stage of transformation are you in?

Development of Fourth Dimensional Thinking

We can choose our own thinking. Nobody can ever control our thinking. Even God does not manipulate our thinking as a man controlling a robot might, or as Satan, our enemy. Neither has anyone the power to do so. There is no one, but ourselves, who can decide what kind of thinking to embrace (Psalm 95:8).

1. Change your self image (2 Corinthians 5:17)

If our self image is not healthy, we cannot think healthy. We should accept and love ourselves, knowing that Christ accepts our biggest weaknesses. This is simply because our status is that of a chosen people, a royal priesthood, a holy nation, and a people belonging to God.

❖ *Tell one another about your self-image.*

2. Get rid of any negative thinking (Ephesians 4:22)

Since the fall of man, negative things control a man's thinking. Unless you remove anger, worry, despair, and anxiety far from you, it becomes a catalyst for further negative energy. Therefore you should reject all negative thinking and be totally repulse by it.

❖ Share with one another what kind of negative thinking is annoying you.

3. Fill your mind with God's thinking. (Psalm 119:11)

Fourth Dimensional Spirituality does not emphasize human thinking. Our thinking should be like God's, not of man's.

Through prayer and meditation, we should accept God's thinking and keep our thinking in check to make sure we are changing it.

❖ Tell one another about your recent prayers and your meditation on God's Word.

4. Fill your present time with creative and positive thinking. (Colossians 3:17)

Today is the best gift God has given us. The positive thinking of today determine tomorrow's positive thinking. There exists a principle of alternation: *man cannot think positively and negatively at the same time.* Therefore, when you cast out negative thinking, you can fill yourself positively with positive thinking. Be relieved with the greater and more creative thinking.

❖ Share with one another how you can make an effort to think positively.

Application and Practice

■ We have studied the Fourth Dimensional Spirituality: Thinking (Application). Share your new understanding with one another.

■ Review the transformation of thinking, and tell one another what benefits may result from it.

■ Talk to each other about what is necessary to develop Fourth Dimensional thinking.

■ Have a time of prayer about becoming a Christian who transforms his self-image into God's image (three minutes).

Key Bible Words
I can do everything through him who gives me strength (Philippians 4:13).

Quote
"There is nothing impossible but only thinking that it's impossible."

— Robert Schuller

Homework
Think about your negative thinking and your negative self-image which has annoyed you. Write down how you can overcome it.

_____

_____

Bibliography
Thinking for a Change by John Maxwell

~Notes~

4

LESSON

Fourth Dimensional Spirituality: Faith

THEORY

The following is a testimony of Cabrera, a South American pastor:
One day a mother came to ask him to lay his hands on her child, who had lost one of his ears. Praying for her son, the pastor saw in faith, God making a beautiful ear for the child. He put his hands on the child, and he prayed earnestly.

As soon as he finished his prayer, the child got a small lump, but not an ear. It looked strange, but the pastor prayed with zeal. Next time, when the boy came again for prayer, he laid his hands on him and prayed with faith, seeing in faith that another ear would be made for him. He kept praying earnestly. He also taught the parents to see in faith that their son already had ears and told them to caress him with that expectation by saying, "My dear baby, you have such beautiful ears." For all the efforts they made, nothing happened.

The next day when they brought the child, the pastor put his hands on him as usual and prayed, still thinking his ears were there. When he opened his eyes, he found that the lump had expanded into a folding fan.

If you first dream of what you want, with faith and in the Spirit, it will come true just as you have imagined.

❖ How are you touched by this story?

_____

_____

_____

_____

_____

❖ Talk to each other about the relationship between faith and miracles.

Check List for Self-assessment of Fourth Dimensional Faith

Though it may not be a perfect standard to determine Fourth Dimensional faith, the checklist below will help you make a good self-assessment. Make sure to assess how closely your faith is aligned to Fourth Dimensional Spirituality with regard to your thinking, beliefs, dreams, and words.

Five points represents the "highest" and one point represents "the lowest" to each question. Circle your answer below:

1. It is a habit to pray and to read Bible everyday.

    1   2   3   4   5

2. I always strive to grow in faith.

    1   2   3   4   5

3. I experience God's guidance more frequently than I expect in most of my daily life.

    1   2   3   4   5

4. I try to solve problems by praying and by meditating on the Word of God, rather than to give myself up to worry.

    1   2   3   4   5

5. I have two or three friends that I pray together with.

    1   2   3   4   5

6. I live on countless resources of God, not on one of mine.

    1   2   3   4   5

7. I believe that God is good and will provide me with more than I ask.

    1   2   3   4   5

8. Thanksgiving, not complaining, comes out of me in times of trouble.

    1   2   3   4   5

9. Once I begin to pray, I do not give up until I get an answer.

    1   2   3   4   5

10. I attend every prayer meeting including early morning prayer and Friday night prayer.

    1   2   3   4   5

Write your total number of points here: My points: (_____)

Results

Over 40 points: You are *full* of the Fourth Dimensional faith.
Keep on with your work until you reach your peak.

30-40 points: You are *average* in Fourth Dimensional faith.
It's time to make an effort to improve your progress.

Below 30 points: You have *little* Fourth Dimensional faith.
Discipline yourself to think about God and focus on Him in all circumstances.

❖ Check your point score total and share with it with one another.

Encounter with the Bible

Please Read Romans 4:16-22:

Therefore, the promise comes by faith, so that it may be by grace and may be guaranteed to all Abraham's offspring—not only to those who are of the law but also to those who are of the faith of Abraham. He is the father of us all. As it is written: "I have made you a father of many nations." He is our father in the sight of God, in whom he believed—the God who gives life to the dead and calls things that are not as though they were. Against all hope, Abraham in hope believed and so became the father of many nations, just as it had been said to him, "So shall your offspring be." Without weakening in his faith, he faced the fact that his body was as good as dead—since he was about a hundred years old—and that Sarah's womb was also dead. Yet he did not waver through unbelief regarding the promise of God, but was strengthened in his faith and gave glory to God, being fully persuaded that God had power to do what he had promised. This is why "it was credited to him as righteousness."

1. The text talks about the faith of Abraham, who is credited as *righteous* by his faith. Who is the God in whom he believed? (v.17)

2. How does the text demonstrate the faith of Abraham, who did not lose it in such a desperate situation? (v.18)

3. What do we believe and trust in when we have faith? (v.20)

4. In seeing what action of Abraham, did God decide to give Abraham the gift of righteousness, which is a sign of having a good relationship with Him? (v.22)

5. Faith enables us to be sure of things that do not seem so certain. Have you ever experienced His power by having hope when things seemed *against* all hope?

   The Scripture says the righteous will live by faith (Habakkuk 2:4). It is faith that we should hold on to in tough situations. Faith holds a very important position in Fourth Dimensional spirituality.

The Significance of Faith

1. Faith sets up your relationship with God.

Faith is essential in your relationship with God. It is impossible to please Him without having faith (Heb 11:6). God communicates and works only with ones who have faith.

Faith Defined by Moses

First 40 years of Moses's life: *He was a great person*
His next 40 years: *He was nothing*
His last 40 years: *God is everything, and he realized this.*

2. Faith is the essence of Christian life.

The foundation of Christian life is to be fulfilled first, secondly, and lastly with faith. Faith is the beginning and essence of Christianity.

Illustration 1:

A large number of people were watching a famous acrobat, Blandine, cross Niagara Falls in 1886. He had crossed it many times. Over the wild waves that were 160 feet high, and falls that were 1,000 feet wide, he crossed on foot, and sometimes even by riding a unicycle. A little boy watched him with wonder. After he completed crossing the falls he said to the boy, "Do you believe that I can cross the falls with a man on this unicycle without his falling off?"

"Certainly, I do believe, sir."

Then he told the boy, "Great, you ride it."

3. Faith expects miracles and produces them.

No matter how much God wants to give us, it would be futile if we do not believe. Faith is a power that brings God's will and heart into effect (John 11:40). Faith is a channel that releases God's power.

4. Faith controls and rules circumstances.

Faith is being sure of what we hope for (Hebrews 11:1). Therefore, we should see what is not visible with the eyes of faith. If we accept His grace with faith, we can enjoy spiritual victory over all kinds of circumstances

5. Faith brings forth courage and vision.

A man of faith does not care about failure and frustration. He has the courage and vision to look past the circumstance and look at the bigger picture (Numbers 13:30).

❖ Share with one another about what is most impressive among the previous five points, with regard to the significance of faith, and give reasons why.

Illustration 2:

What do you think General MacArthur thought to himself when he had no choice but to abandon the Philippines? He said, "I surely will come back," and he really believed that he would. He announced this when the U.S. Pacific fleet had suffered a major defeat and the Japanese had occupied most of the South Pacific. His statement was full of confidence and conviction. As it turned out, he really did come back.

My Strength + Power of Faith = Power of Faith—*My strength*

Application and Practice

■ We have studied the Fourth Dimensional Spirituality: Faith (Theory). Share with one another anything new you have learned?

■ Review the section "The Significance of Faith" and share with one another about the significance of faith.

■ Share with one another regarding the miracles you have experienced through the faith that God has given each one of you.

■ Spend some time in prayer. Pray that you will live with faith, which enables us to overcome the world (three minutes).

Key Bible Words

And without faith it is impossible to please God, because anyone who comes to Him must believe that He exists and that He rewards those who earnestly seek Him (Hebrews 11:6).

Quote

"Faith is participating in the deepest joy of heaven even though I walk the thorny path of my life, because I know His love towards me is immeasurable."

—Pamela Reeve

Homework

Write a devotional essay based on your daily prayer life and daily meditation on God's Word.

_____

_____

_____

_____

_____

_____

_____

_____

_____

_____

_____

_____

_____

_____

_____

_____

_____

_____

_____

_____

_____

_____

_____

_____

Bibliography

Authentic Faith by Gary Thomas

Fourth Dimensional Spirituality: Faith

APPLICATION

Along time ago, a new church was planted on the fourth floor of a five-story building. There was no problem in the Sunday morning services, but serious problems occurred during the night services. There was a bar located right above the church, on the fifth floor. Thus, when people sang praise in the church, they would hear another song from the bar above. When they sang "Amazing Grace," they heard the lyrics, "I do not know your name, but…." When they sang, "I'm called…" with a strong tone, they heard "Who loves…" in an even stronger tone. Under this condition, it was impossible to have a worship service.Desperate, the pastor made up his mind to pray for a month, wishing that the bar would be removed. After twenty-five days, a fire broke out in the bar. Only the bar on the fifth floor was burned completely. The church and the restaurant were saved from the fire and not even a curtain was burned. The owner of the bar heard that the pastor had prayed wishing for the bar to be removed and accused him to the police. Eventually, the pastor was called in for investigation.

"Pastor, I am sorry to trouble you, but the owner of the bar told us that the fire broke out because you prayed for it to happen. Is it true?"

"Yes, it is true that I prayed, wishing for the bar to be removed. However, do you think is it possible that a fire can break out through somebody's prayer?"

"Pastor, it is strange. The owner of the bar believes in the power of prayer, and you don't? The police report was as follows: "The fire did not break out because of such a faithless pastor."

❖ How do you think you would have reacted if you were the pastor in this situation?

_____

_____

_____

_____

_____

How Faith Is Born

Faith is not born in a day. You should make a constant effort to develop faith. Here are some prayer steps you should take to bring faith to life.

1. Picture the object clearly in your mind.
Since faith is the substance of things hoped for, we need to have a clear goal. *No prayer is answered if a goal is aimless and not clear.*

❖ Write down a list of prayers and make your object clear:

Name: _____

Resolution: _____

Subject of Prayers:

1. _____
2. _____
3. _____
4. _____
5. _____

The need: _____

The period: _____

Analyzing prayer request date: _____

Ways to accomplish: _____

Importance of accomplishing it: _____

For whose benefit? _____

List of rewards	Obstacles	How to Overcome?
1. _____	_____	_____
2. _____	_____	_____
3. _____	_____	_____
4. _____	_____	_____
5. _____	_____	_____

Date of Completion:	Month / Day / Year	Period of Completion
1. _____	_____	_____
2. _____	_____	_____
3. _____	_____	_____
4. _____	_____	_____
5. _____	_____	_____

❖ *Related Scripture: (Mark 9:23)*

2. Have a strong desire.

After you decide what the subject of the prayer is, you need to embrace it with a burning desire. Moreover, you should keep looking at the image of a completed goal, with faith.

3. Pray that you would acquire assurance.

Faith is the substance of things hoped for. In Greek, "substance" means *hypostasis*, which means *deed or substance, essence, and assurance*. Therefore, we should continue to pray until we have the assurance of faith.

4. Prove your faith.

If you have assurance, you have to show proof of your faith. At this stage, speaking with faith is very important. If we pray until we have assurance and state our goal with the words of faith, assurance will appear right before our eyes.

Encounter with the Bible

Read Mark 9:21-29:

> *Jesus asked the boy's father, "How long has he been like this?" "From childhood," he answered. "It has often thrown him into fire or water to kill him. But if you can do anything, take pity on us and help us." "'If you can'?" said Jesus. "Everything is possible for him who believes." Immediately the boy's father exclaimed, "I do believe; help me overcome my unbelief!" When Jesus saw that a crowd was running to the scene, he rebuked the evil spirit. "You deaf and mute spirit," he said, "I command you, come out of him and never enter him again." The spirit shrieked, convulsed him violently and came out. The boy looked so much like a corpse that many said, "He's dead." But Jesus took him by the hand and lifted him to his feet, and he stood up. After Jesus had gone indoors, his disciples asked him privately, "Why couldn't we drive it out?" He replied, "This kind can come out only by prayer."*

1. The background of the text is after *Jesus was transformed before three disciples*, while the other nine disciples were ridiculed severely because they could not heal the demon-possessed boy. How did the demon harm the child? (v.22)

_____

_____

_____

_____

_____

2. Why did Jesus indirectly say to his disciples that they could not heal the demon-possessed boy? (v23)

_____

_____

_____

3. What order did Jesus give to the demon? (v.25)

_____

_____

_____

4. Regarding the source of power, what did Jesus reply to his disciples when they asked him about the miracle they had just witnessed? (v.29)

_____

_____

_____

5. What do you think of the relationship between faith and prayer?

_____

_____

_____

❖ Share with one another.

Everyone has a measure of faith (Romans 12:3). We can be good servants of God when we utilize our faith in accordance with the measure of faith that God has given us.

We should know how to make good use of it in order to achieve the goal of glorifying God. Wholesome and well-balanced faith is possible when the blood of Jesus, anointing of the Spirit, and the word of God are held together closely,

Four Ways to Develop Fourth Dimensional Faith

One who is saved by the blood of Jesus, empowered by the anointing of the Spirit, and devoted to the word of God will live a victorious Christian life. We should especially arm ourselves with the blood of Jesus. The blood of Jesus forgives sins, cures diseases, casts out demons, conquers the curse of circumstances, and purifies our conscience and belief.

❖ Share with one another if you have ever experienced the power of the blood of Jesus.

How to be armed with the blood of Jesus:

> Be cleansed by the blood of Jesus.
> Put the blood of Jesus upon you.
> Drink the blood of Jesus.
> Sprinkle the blood of Jesus and be covered by it.

1. To Develop Fourth Dimensional Faith: Be Anointed with the Holy Spirit

Unless one is filled with the Spirit, his faith does not grow. The anointing of the Spirit takes place through impartation, training, and prayer. We can live a strong Christian life only with the supernatural gifts of the Spirit. The gift of faith, as a gift of the Spirit, is the power of trusting God in impossible situations. With the gift of faith, we can gain the confidence and assurance that will allow us to be victorious over our circumstances.

❖ *Have you experienced a greater sense of confidence ever since you received the gift of faith in your life?*

_____

_____

_____

_____

_____

2. To Develop Fourth Dimensional Faith: Equip Yourself with the Word of God

The Scripture is the absolute, truthful word of God. We can trust the Bible because it contains a unified massage, and it is formed in solidarity.

John 5:39:

> *You search the Scriptures, for in them you think you have eternal life; and these are they which testify of Me.*

❖ According to the above Scripture, through whom can we possess eternal life?

_____

_____

Implement the Five Fingers of God's Word for Study

After studying the Five Fingers of God's Word listed below, try to apply them in your life. What are the "five fingers of God's Word?" Below is a list and then a Scripture illuminating the meaning of each study principle. You will find them a wonderful asset to your spiritual growth.

1. Read

2. Memorize

3. Meditate

4. Hear

5. Practice

Read:

Then Philip ran up to the chariot and heard the man reading Isaiah. "Do you understand what you are reading?" Philip asked (Acts 8:30).

Memorize:

"These commandments that I give you today are to be upon your hearts" (Deuteronomy 6:6).

Meditate:

"Oh, how I love your law! I meditate on it all day long" (Psalm119:97).

Hear:

"I will listen to what God the LORD will say; He promises peace to His people, His saints— but let them not return to folly" (Psalm 85:8).

Practice:

"Therefore everyone who hears these words of mine and puts them into practice is like a wise man who builds his house upon a rock" (Matthew 7:24).

Why We Study and Practice God's Word

"For Ezra had devoted himself to the study and observance of the Law of the LORD, and to teaching its decrees and laws in Israel" (Ezra 7:10).

3. To Develop Fourth Dimensional Faith: Minister with Faith

As much we need exercise to maintain our physical health, we need to serve others and spread the Gospel in order to make our faith healthy. A healthy church is a church whose members work and minister.

Your devotion and effort will soundly build up your church. Scripture indicates that the characteristics of a healthy church are: Jesus as the head of the church; a well-functioning leadership for ministry and growth; a church as a community of spiritual ministry; and growth of the church in both quality and in quantity (Ephesians 4:11-12).

❖ Share with one another if you have experienced great progress in your belief through the ministry of faith.

Application and Practice

■ We have studied Fourth Dimensional Spirituality: Faith (Application). Share with one another if you have learned anything new.

■ Review "Developing Fourth Dimensional Faith," and share with one another about why we can trust the Word of God.

■ Review the Five Fingers illustration of God's Word and share with one another about how we can apply it in our lives.

■ Have a time of prayer. Pray about becoming a mature Christian who serves the Church and evangelizes through faith (three minutes).

Key Bible Words
"If you can?" said Jesus. "Everything is possible for him who believes" (Mark 9:23).

Quote
"The vision concerning the church does not come from the outside. It arises within him through faith."

—Dr. David Yonggi Cho

Homework
Write a testimony about experiencing blessing through prayer and relying on the blood of Jesus.

_____

_____

_____

_____

_____

_____

_____

_____

_____

Bibliography
Faithful Thinking, Faith to Act by Gordon McDonald

~Notes~

Fourth Dimensional Spirituality: Dreams

THEORY

There was a young man in New York who had a dream to build a bridge connecting Brooklyn to Manhattan across the river in eastern New York. When he stressed that he would suspend the bridge in the air, all the people regarded his plan as an impossible dream. However, he confidently persisted to find some supporters so that he could finally start working.

One day, a tragic accident occurred, which crippled him for life. He could not walk at all and had to stay at his apartment. However, he did not give up, but appointed his son to be director of the project. Because he could see the construction area, he supervised his son, watching the entire progress with a telescope.

Finally, by 1883, the famous Brooklyn Bridge had been completed in fourteen years by constructor John Roebling and his son. It was completed according to the design and dream of Mr. Roebling

❖ *Have you ever achieved a great accomplishment by an unyielding effort, embracing a dream in your own life?*

Check List for Self-assessment of Fourth Dimensional Dreams

Although the following list may not be the absolute in standard to assess your progress in Fourth Dimensional dreams, this list will help you closely align yourself to Fourth Dimensional Spirituality with regard to your thinking, beliefs, dreams, and words.

Five points represents the "highest" and one point represents "the lowest" to each question. Circle your answer below:

1. I am aware of the vision and gift of the Spirit that God has given me.

        1   2   3   4   5

2. I occasionally check whether or not my desire it is in accord with the scripture, rather than my own personal greed.

        1   2   3   4   5

3. I pray and prepare myself to one day achieve my dream.
    1   2   3   4   5

4. I share my dream with people around me and ask for prayer.
    1   2   3   4   5

5. I always try to give shape to my dream.
    1   2   3   4   5

6. I do my best even in the small things in order to fulfill my dream.
    1   2   3   4   5

7. I always try to have a dream that is bigger than my ability.
    1   2   3   4   5

8. Though I suffer from failing at my dream, I keep praying with patience.
    1   2   3   4   5

9. I record my dream and read it over and over to keep my dream in my mind.
    1   2   3   4   5

10. I believe that my dream will come true, and I will rely on the Holy Spirit.
    1   2   3   4   5

Write your total number of points here: My points: (_____)

Results
Over 40 points:
You are *full* of Fourth Dimensional Dreams.
Keep on with your work until you reach perfection.

30-40 points:
You are of *average* in Fourth Dimensional Dreams.
It's time to make a greater effort and progress.

Below 30 points:
You have *little* Fourth Dimensional Dreams.
Try to receive *God's dream* through prayer.

❖ Check your point total and share with each one another.

Encounter with the Bible

Please Read Joel 2:27-32:

Then you will know that I am in Israel, that I am the LORD your God, and that there is no other; never again will my people be shamed. And afterward, I will pour out my Spirit on all people. Your sons and daughters will prophesy, your old men will dream dreams, your young men will see visions. Even on my servants, both men and women, I will pour out my Spirit in those days. I will show wonders in the heavens and on the earth, blood and fire and billows of smoke. The sun will be turned to darkness and the moon to blood before the coming of the great and dreadful day of the LORD. And everyone who calls on the name of the LORD will be saved; for on Mount Zion and in Jerusalem there will be deliverance, as the LORD has said, among the survivors whom the LORD calls.

1. The text is about a prophecy that Joel, a prophet, received, regarding a revelation that God's blessings will be poured out in the last days. What will the believers not experience in the Last Days? (v.27)

   _____

   _____

   _____

2. What is the gift that God has prepared for all people in the Last Days? (v.28)

   _____

   _____

   _____

3. What is the result of the outpouring of the Holy Spirit on the following?

   a. Children

   _____

   b. Old men

   _____

   c. Young men

   _____

4. Who will be saved in the Last Days? (v. 32)

   _____

   _____

5. When the Holy Spirit is poured out, we will dream dreams. It is said that "visions" and "dreams" are languages of the Holy Spirit. What kind of vision have you received through the Holy Spirit?

_____

_____

_____

Great things are mostly conceived first in one's heart before they are displayed in reality.
Dreams and visions in one's heart are very precious assets powerful enough to create reality.

God's Dreams and Man's Dreams

Dreams in Fourth Dimensional Spirituality do not coincide with just having a *personal ambition.* Sometimes we consider personal desire and ambition as a dream given by God. We should be careful to discern correctly; it is our greed which we should watch out for (Colossians 3:5).

Fourth Dimensional Spirituality dreams refer to *God-given dreams.* We can have God's vision *only after we throw away our personal dreams* originating from our greed. When we discard all of *our* greed, and try to listen to God's voice, we can possess the dream which the Holy Spirit bestows upon us.

❖   Share with one another from the point of view of God's dreams versus man's dreams by looking at the story of Moses. Moses initially failed to save his people by himself, but later succeeded in leading them in the Exodus after he had an encounter with God.

The Significance of God's Dream

Below are gauges by which we can discern the reality of a dream from God versus a selfish and man-devised dream:

1. A dream from God lets us have a clear goal.

Scripture says where there is no revelation, the people cast off restraint (Proverbs 29:18). A dream is like a signpost, which leads our lives. One who has a dream can live a purpose-driven life.

2. A dream from God lets us say "I can" with confidence.

I come to think about my potential and make an effort to show my ability the most when I have dream. After finding out the great potential within me, I have a confidence within me never realized before

3. A dream from God leads us to have passion for life.

The lifestyle between the one who has a dream and the one who does not is quite different. The former faces a matter passionately, while the other is inclined to stay idle. This kind of dream is a living force, arousing enthusiasm for life.

4. A dream from God lets us look forward to a creative future.

In the Greek, "human" means *one who looks up.* Man is *one who looks up* and embraces a dream. A "dream" from God is a bridge linking present to future and that with which we can create a productive future.

5. A dream from God energizes our lives.

A dream allows us to have a clear goal, which enables us to concentrate our energy to live effectively. If we concentrate our energy on one direction, our power will be much greater.

❖ Share with one another regarding the significance of a God's *dream.*

Another Self-assessment

The following assessment asks us questions from in-depth principles critical to determine the right dream. For a dream to be God's dream, it must be linked to ten principles. Apply these ten principles of dream-making to your life.

Tips: Ten Principles of Dream-making

We need in-depth principles for dream-making in order to know which is the right dream. My dream must be linked closely to *these* principles. Now take this assessment. A score of five points represents the "highest" and one point represents "the lowest" to each question. Circle your answers below:

1. Try to find out your lifetime task. To find a dream is to find a life, just like finding gold in the field.

                    1 2 3 4 5

Reason: _____

2. Analyze where your dream is heading.

                    1 2 3 4 5

Reason: _____

3. State clearly "why I should have a dream like this."

                    1 2 3 4 5

Reason: _____

4. Analyze how important your dream will be in the future for your neighbor and for yourself.

                    1 2 3 4 5

Reason: _____

5. Analyze for whom you have to keep your dream.

                1 2 3 4 5

Reason: _____

6. Catch on *how* you can fulfill the dream.

                1 2 3 4 5

Reason: _____

7. Find a partner to work together with to fulfill the dream.

                1 2 3 4 5

Reason: _____

8. Find a motive to revive your dream when it withers.

                1 2 3 4 5

Reason: _____

9. Establish the formula of your dream.

                1 2 3 4 5

Reason: _____

10. Let all your goals be toward accomplishing your dream.

                1 2 3 4 5

Reason: _____

Application and Practice

We have now studied the Fourth Dimensional Spirituality: Dream (Theory). Do the following individual or group exercise:

■ Share with one another if you have learned anything new.

■ Share with one another if you have ever confused personal desire with God's dream.

■ Share with one another regarding the significance and power of having a dream that you have experienced by applying the ten principles of dream-making.

■ Spend some time in prayer that you will be a Christian who works hard to fulfill the dream that God gives you (three minutes).

Key Bible Words

Where there is no revelation, the people cast off restraint; but blessed is he who keeps the law (Proverbs 29:18).

Quote

"Do not negotiate for a dream. It must soar up to the sky freely."

— Jesse Jackson

Homework

Write down five visions for your next ten years:

1. _____

2. _____

3. _____

4. _____

5. _____

Bibliography

Design Your Dream by Kyung Jik Shin

~Notes~

Fourth Dimensional Spirituality: Dreams

APPLICATION

There was a boy. He was a below average student, and the other children made fun of him. He liked bustling around with a 8mm camera much more than reading a book. He quit school when he was in the eleventh grade, but his parents persuaded him to go back to school. When he came back to school, he was sent to the class for *slow learners.* He only stayed in that class for one month because soon after, his family moved to another city where he graduated from a high school that was a better fit for him. He was rejected by a regular movie school, and reluctantly attended another college and majored in English. Afterward, the direction of his future suddenly changed.

He went to Universal Studios, where he met Chuck Silvers, who was one of the top executives working in the editorial department. Silvers loved the boy because the young man was already making movies at his young age. He invited him to "come back later (when he was older).

The young boy came into the Universal Studios building without any pass or specific reason. However, the dream in his heart for film-making was so fervent that it did not matter to him. During that entire summer, he hung around the many directors and script writers. At times, he even sat in an empty office and stayed there without permission.

Years passed, and when the boy was twenty-eight years old, he made a movie that became a worldwide blockbuster, grossing 470 million dollars. At the time, it was the largest grossing film in history. He continued to make movies and won many awards. He became a movie director who is recognized worldwide because he never gave up his dream. This boy's name was Steven Spielberg.

❖   *What do you think is necessary for you to achieve your dream?*

Dream Achievers

There are a number of *dream achievers.* One thing they have in common is that they set sound goals. Looking at their cases, we can learn some good methods and attitudes to have for setting a goal.

Freud and Viktor Frankl's Goals

Psychologist Sigmond Freud said, "Setting a goal is dangerous, because pride is damaged if you fail." But the psychiatrist Viktor Frankl said," No goal is more dangerous than an unachieved goal."

Our ministry supports Dr. Frankl's statement without hesitation.

Paul Meyer's Goal Theory

"The key to success is setting a goal. I can affirm that 75 percent of my success is because of setting goals. A dream is a static thought and a goal is a dynamic action."

Son Jung-ik's Goal

Jung-ik Son, the foremost venture businessman in Japan, set his goal early in life. A hitch-hiking trip across the western United States when he was in the tenth grade changed his fate. In the wide-open land, amidst the fresh air, he set his goal of becoming a prominent businessman in this world. Just at that moment he set his life-time goal of "Winning fame in my twenties; being a billionaire in my thirties; making a full effort in my forties; getting ready to retire from the business in my fifties; and turning the business over to my successor in my sixties."

Rockefeller's Goal

Rockefeller, a billionaire oil businessman, set a goal, "For me, for money," when he was young. However he was diagnosed with a serious disease, and his flesh was rotting. In the midst of his trouble, he met God. While he was recovering from bad health, he changed his goal to "For God, for Mankind." As stated in his goal, he raked in money through the oil business and donated large sums of it to charity until he reached ninety-eight years of age.

A Goal is a chariot carrying one's life.

Encounter with the Bible

Read Gen 13:14-18:

The LORD said to Abram after Lot had parted from him, "Lift up your eyes from where you are and look north and south, east and west. All the land that you see I will give to you and your offspring forever. I will make your offspring like the dust of the earth, so that if anyone could count the dust, then your offspring could be counted. Go, walk through the length and breadth of the land, for I am giving it to you." So Abram moved his tents and went to live near the great trees of Mamre at Hebron, where he built an altar to the LORD.

1. The text contains the story of God confirming the promise that Abram (later renamed Abraham) "would be a blessing." What did God command Abraham to do after Lot had left him?

2. God gives two promises to Abraham. What are they? (v.15,16)

   1. _____

   2. _____

3. How did Abraham give glory to God when he received God's promise? (v.18)

   _____

   _____

4. God gave Abraham a promise/dream of being a father of many nations. He told him to look north and south and east and west so that he could envision that dream. "Seeing it afar off" and picturing what God had said, Abraham dreamed that his descendants would be as many as there are stars in the heavens. Do you practice daily seeing in faith the vision that God has given you?

   We should live with the holy dream that God gives to us. A dream in itself is amazingly powerful to build up our lives. If this is true, how, then, can we develop the God-given Forth Dimensional Dream?

How to Develop a Fourth Dimensional Dream

   Take the steps below, that you might develop a Fourth Dimensional Dream in your life:

1. Pray in the name of Jesus and in the power of the Spirit for God's dream to be placed within your heart.

   A Forth Dimensional Dream is not a human ambition, but rather a holy vision that God gives.

   Therefore, above all, we should pray in the name of Jesus, that God will place His dream and svision within us. When we pray, dreaming in our hearts that God' great and unreachable dream will happen, God will work beyond our imaginations (Jeremiah 33:3).

❖   If you have ever experienced a desire to receive a great, God-given vision through prayer, share it with one another.

2. Have a God-directed dream and goal that is *concise* to you.

   A dream does not show its head on the clouds and blow around in the wind. Our dream should be clear, real, and specific. There are six principles in setting a dream. *They are:*

   1. Where—the direction,

   2. What—the significance,

   3. When—the time to achieve,

   4. How—the method,

   5. Why—the reason to achieve, and

   6. Whom—the beneficiary.

❖   *Evaluate your dream according to the six principles listed above.*

3.   Begin with the small things if you want to achieve a dream. A dream can be fulfilled when we begin with the small things. Somebody said, "Think big and act small." Put into practice the small things first, even though you may have a big dream. One who is faithful in the small things can do great things.

❖   *Share with one another about the small, but specific goals that will allow you to fulfill your dream.*

4.   Establish your dream with a combination of your knowledge, connections, network, and experiences.
    It is important to equip ourselves with necessary knowledge these days. Today is an era of connection and networking. It is necessary to learn how to work together, not relying on your own strength. All kinds of experiences, not only from a direct source but also indirect ones, such as books and movies, enrich our lives.

❖   *Think about how you can utilize your knowledge and network you've built through your experiences.*

5.   Never give up. Rather, move on. When we are in pursuit of a dream, sometimes we may come face-to-face with failure and frustration. But remember, *failure is a signpost for achievement.* To achieve a dream, we need to know how to enjoy the process of fulfillment, which takes our entire life.

❖   *Fill in the Goal and Dream Table to demonstrates what you think your dream will be ten years from now. Next, write down three obstacles to your dream, as well as the way to overcome the obstacles.*

Goal and Dream Table

Remember:
- It is possible!
- Set your goal!
- If you do, then you will know it!
- Everything is possible for him who believes.

Name: _____Date: _____

Email: _____ Phone: _____

Date of Accomplishing Goal/Dream: _____

Dream: _____

Top 5 Goals—Lifetime Mission:

1. _____
2. _____
3. _____
4. _____
5. _____

Reward of fulfilled dream: _____

_____

Obstacles you need to handle: _____

_____

Three ways to overcome them:

1. _____
2. _____
3. _____

My Decision:

_____

_____

Application and Practice

- ◼ We have studied Forth Dimensional Spirituality: Dreams (application).

- ◼ Share with one another if you have learned anything new.

- ◼ Review the section "Developing Fourth Dimensional Dreams" and share with one another about specific goals through which your dream will be fulfilled.

- ◼ Share with one another about your interchanging network and your various experiences.

- ◼ Spend some time in prayer; that you will become a Christian who is used by God through a vision that God gives you (three minutes).

Key Bible Words

And afterward, I will pour out my Spirit on all people. Your sons and daughters will prophesy, your old men will dream dreams, your young men will see visions (Joel 2:28).

Quote

"Tell me about your vision, and I will prophesy your future."

—Dr. David Yonggi Cho

Homework

Set ten goals for your church, and draw a timetable about the plan of progress.

	Goals	Timetable of Progress
1.	_____	_____
2.	_____	_____
3.	_____	_____
4.	_____	_____
5.	_____	_____
6.	_____	_____
7.	_____	_____
8.	_____	_____
9.	_____	_____
10.	_____	_____

Bibliography

Blue Ocean of My Life by Dr. Chong Woon Kwak

~Notes~

Fourth Dimensional Spirituality: Words

THEORY

Billy Graham is the most world renown evangelist of the 20th Century. We can say we are blessed to have lived in the same generation with such a great evangelist. However during his childhood, he was a brat, making all his neighbors frown. They shook their heads saying, "What an earth will he end up like?"

Only his grandmother said differently. Caressing her rascal grandson, she said, "You are good at words and winning over people. You will succeed greatly if you develop your character." That single comment changed his life, and he eventually became a world-known evangelist.

General MacArthur was a bully too. He caused many kids a lot of trouble. People were really anxious about his future. Nevertheless, his grandmother said, "You are a born soldier." Afterwards, he confessed that he was awakened by this. Eventually, he became a great soldier.

One single word of praise can change the course of one man's life.

❖ *Have you ever seen some people changing the course of their lives because of your single word?*

Check List for Self-assessment of the Fourth Dimensional Words

Though it may not be a perfect standard for measuring Fourth Dimensional Words, use the checklist below for self-assessment. This will help you determine how closely your words are aligned to Fourth Dimensional Spirituality, among your thinking, beliefs, dreams, *and words.*

Five points represents the "highest" and one point represents "the lowest" to each question. Circle your answer below:

1. I try to quote Scripture or use biblical language while praying or conversing.

             1   2   3   4   5

2. I encourage and compliment others.

             1   2   3   4   5

3. I think through before I speak, in consideration of the other party.
       1   2   3   4   5

4. When I speak, I constantly use positive words.
       1   2   3   4   5

5. I do not use negative words even when I face unexpected situations.
       1   2   3   4   5

6. I say positive statements about myself.
       1   2   3   4   5

7. I pray that the statements I make about myself will be fulfilled.
       1   2   3   4   5

8. I believe that the authority and power of words can determine my life.
       1   2   3   4   5

9. I have experienced a change in my life by changing my words.
       1   2   3   4   5

10. Even when everything goes wrong, I do not lose faith.

Write down your total.
       1   2   3   4   5

Write your total number of points here: My points: (_____)

Results
Over 40 points: You are *full* of Fourth Dimensional words.
Keep on with your work until you become perfect.

30-40 points:
You are of average in Fourth Dimensional Words.
It's time to make an effort to improve your progress.

Below 30 points:
You have *little* of Fourth Dimensional Words.
Try to speak more positively.

❖ Check your total score and share it with one another.

Encounter with the Bible

Please Read Job 2:6-10:

*The LORD said to Satan, "Very well, then, he is in your hands; but you must spare his life."
So Satan went out from the presence of the LORD and afflicted Job with painful sores from
the soles of his feet to the top of his head. Then Job took a piece of broken pottery and
scraped himself with it as he sat among the ashes. His wife said to him, "Are you still holding
on to your integrity? Curse God and die!" He replied, "You are talking like a foolish
woman. Shall we accept good from God, and not trouble?" In all this, Job did not sin in
what he said.*

1. The text is about an incident in which Job suffered a calamity of painful sores caused by the
test of Satan. After a close look at the text, in what condition do you think Satan's test takes place?
(v.6)

_____

_____

_____

2. What did Job's wife instigate Job to do when he was tormented and in anguish by what Satan
brought him? (v.9)

_____

_____

_____

3. Job replied wisely to his wife. According to him, *from whom* do all the blessings and curses of
life come?

_____

_____

_____

4. Job did not sin in what he said, "Shall we accept good from God, and not trouble?" When did
you try not to sin with your lips in your difficulties?

_____

_____

_____

Man and words are inseparable. Man carries out his social life by expressing his mind through words. Words are also one of the essential elements of Fourth Dimensional Spirituality. Words are a path of power to change our third dimensional life.

Words and God's Creation

Words are a very important factor in God's creation. God spoke, and there was creation (Genesis 1:3). God's Word has creative power.

In this way, man's words, though they are not perfect, share the same kind of creative power. If we speak negatively, negative things happen. When we speak positively, positive things happen. Thus, words in the power of the Holy Spirit have amazing power to control and transform our lives.

❖ *Share with one another if you have experienced something ever happening according to your words.*

The Authority of Words and the Holy Spirit

As a boomerang comes back to the one who throws it, the words of the speaker come back to the speaker. A word that comes out of someone's mouth not only has an effect on his neighbor, but it also returns to have the same effect on himself. Words affect you greatly as well as your neighbor (Proverbs 12:14). Because words have power, they should be under control.

The best teacher is the Holy Spirit. If you react sensitively to Him and let the Spirit guide you in what to say in a critical situation, you will save a lot of embarrassment and failure (Matthew 10:20).

❖ *Share with each other if you have ever experienced the Holy Spirit guiding you in what to say in an urgent situation or when evangelizing to unbelievers.*

Significance of Words

1. Words control life.

A single word can either kill or save a man. While a sword can be used to kill one man at a time, a word is even stronger than a sword. It is explosive like an atomic bomb in that it can be used as a weapon to destroy a number of people in an instant.

❖ *Share with each other if you have ever experienced that life and death are separated by words.*

2. Words control an environment.

When *Fortune Magazine* surveyed the executives of the world's best 500 enterprises, 94 percent of them had picked internal attitude as a primary factor for their success. Thoughts and words are important characteristics of internal attitude. Words can change our environment, enabling us to be more productive.

We need word techniques to influence our environment effectively. Can you make use of edification, pointing out and encouraging appropriately?

3. Words can control your physical body.

Words affect physical functioning also. It happens that a doctor's erroneous statement, "It is incurable" leads to death in a patient. A doctor's words become known to the patient, make the patient lose heart, and eventually lead to the deterioration of his physical condition.

❖ *Share with each other if you have ever experienced your body reacting to words.*

4. Words are a vehicle of spiritual authority.

Words have spiritual authority. A proclamation of faith in what God has said has the power to make what you hope for happen in reality. Faith exercises its power through a path called proclamation. How does the following Scripture say we can be saved?

For with the heart a person believes, resulting in righteousness, and with the mouth he confesses, resulting in salvation (Romans 10:10).

5. Words bring forth the transformation of an organization.

Words create change in an organization. The competence of a company will be maximized when it has one common goal and vision. Just as an athlete yells "Go for it!" before playing a game, the transformation of an organization will be accelerated when its goal and vision are expressed verbally.

Application and Practice

■ We have studied the Fourth Dimensional Spirituality: Words (theory). Share with one another if you have learned anything new.

■ Consider any specific ways that the Holy Spirit can guide your words.

■ Share with one another about which among the five points regarding the significance of words is most impressive, and also give reasons to support your answer.

■ Have a time of prayer that words will change your life and exercise a good influence on others (three minutes).

Key Bible Words

Pleasant words are a honeycomb, sweet to the soul and healing to the bones (Proverbs 16:24).

Quote

"Your life will be just like you speak."

—Dr. David Yonggi Cho

Homework

Make a list of ten positive traits about yourself and say them aloud ten times a day.

1. _____
2. _____
3. _____
4. _____
5. _____

6. _____
7. _____
8. _____
9. _____
10. _____

Bibliography

Your Words Create Miracles by Phil Park

~Notes~

9

LESSON

Fourth Dimensional Spirituality: Words

APPLICATION

Years ago, a woman came down with an illness. At first she seemed to have a common cold, but the condition worsened. Eventually, she felt so terrible that her heart began to beat really fast, and she became very dizzy and fell into a coma. Nine days later, she regained consciousness. After the examination, she was diagnosed with terminal lymphatic cancer. She confessed her sins in tears and prayed, "I will live for You if You save my life." She took anticancer therapy, but she only got worse. The doctors finally gave her family notice to start preparing for her funeral.

They gave up; however she did not give up. As she kept listening to the audio sermon in the hospital room, she repented and prayed continually. One day, when she was listening to a message, she was deeply touched by the Word: "Where, O death, is your victory? Where, O death, is your sting?" She accepted the words and proclaimed, "Yes. Where, O death within me is your victory? Where, O death, is your sting? I am healed in the name of Jesus. I have a victory through His blood. Get out, you death!" After that, she started to resist fearlessly. Whenever a nurse gave her a shot, she said to herself, "By His wounds I am healed."

At that time, she sensed her entire body being healed by the ministry of the Holy Spirit and excitedly ran to the hospital. She was reexamined, and there was no sign of lymphatic cancer! As a result of this miracle, her unbelieving husband and his whole family repented, and miraculously, they all believed in Jesus.

❖ *Have you ever experienced any of your problems being solved through fearless proclamation of God's Word on your lips?*

Commendation Changes Fate

In the early 1800s, there was a little boy who was behind in his writing ability. It was not until he was eleven years old that he wrote something that someone would say "looked like writing," only to be ridiculed. A lady told him, "I'd better look after other things instead of reading your work."

Extremely discouraged, he came back home, and his mother gave him a flower and told him,

53

"Your writing has yet to blossom. But don't worry; your day is coming." This unskilled boy later on went to become a great writer.

The Commandments of Commendation
 Below are listed the ten commandments of commendation which you would do well to implement in your relationships with others:

1. Commend right away when something commendable happens.
2. Commend good work.
3. Commend in public if possible.
4. Commend a process rather than a result.
5. Commend as you would commend your lover.
6. Avert falsehood and commend truthfully.
7. Positive eyes search for what is commendable.
8. Encourage all the more when things are not going well.
9. When something bad happens to someone, move his concern to another direction.
10. Occasionally, commend yourself.

Encounter with the Bible

Please Read Numbers 14:24-30:
 "But because my servant Caleb has a different spirit and follows me wholeheartedly, I will bring him into the land he went to, and his descendants will inherit it. Since the Amalekites and Canaanites are living in the valleys, turn back tomorrow and set out toward the desert along the route to the Red Sea." The LORD said to Moses and Aaron: "How long will his wicked community grumble against me? I have heard the complaints of these grumbling Israelites. So tell them, As surely as I live, declares the LORD, I will do to you the very things I heard you say: In this desert your bodies will fall—every one of you twenty years old or more who was counted in the census and who has grumbled against me. Not one of you will enter the land I swore with uplifted hand to make your home, except Caleb son of Jephunneh and Joshua son of Nun."

1. The Scripture text is about God's wrath on the twelve spies for reporting some information to the people of Israel, after they had returned from Canaan. What was the punishment that God gave to the Israelites who were on the brink of entering Canaan? (v.25)

_____

_____

2. What specific behavior did God *not* tolerate? (v.27)

_____

_____

_____

3. God said He would do exactly what the Israelites had spoken. What was His punishment to the people of Israel? (v.29)

_____

_____

4. What was the reason Caleb and Joshua could enter the promise land? (v.30)

_____

_____

5. God showed that He brings to pass what we speak and what He hears in line with His Word. Did you ever realize that your words have such authority?

_____

_____

_____

Words offer us unlimited possibility, but at the same time, they have tremendous power to be able to ruin our destiny. Scripture says, "If anyone is never at fault in what he says, he is a perfect man, able to keep his whole body in check" (James 3:2). How can we develop Fourth Dimensional words, which have such amazing authority?

How to Develop Fourth Dimensional Words

1. Speak with positive and creative words.

God's words in our mouth, have the power to make what we speak happen, so we should talk positively and creatively. A righteous man always speaks with appropriate, wise, useful, and life-giving words. This is a good influence on him as well as on others.

❖ *How much do you try to use creative and successful words?*

2. Confirm to yourself that "you can."

The capacity of the human brain is so large that it is the equivalent of 1,000 computers, ten billion micro-film cartridges, copier machines, cameras, videos, and widescreen projectors. It is well beyond our imagination.

God gave us great ability. However, we do not make use of it creatively. Since we are believers living on the unlimited power of God, we should have positive thinking and proclaim, "I can" with our lips.

3. Speak a word containing compliments and encouragement.

Compliments and encouragement have amazing power to motivate other people. Keep in mind that a single word of encouragement can change the fate of others. Compliments and encouragement are Fourth Dimensional languages that have the power to determine or influence a destiny.

❖ *Share with each other about what is the most common compliment you give to others.*

4. Improve your communication skills.

Communication is so important in today's society. If I want to achieve Fourth dimensional words, I need the ability to deliver my thinking clearly. It is through communication that we can influence each other.

❖ *Share with one another about what you are doing to improve your communication skills.*

5. Make use of powerful words.

Words have the power to control one's entire life. Therefore, we need to know and make good use of the authority of words. Words have power within themselves, and we should try to bear fruit by saying positive and powerful words.

Examples of positive words. (Fill in the blanks):

I will do _____

I can do _____

I will go through with _____

I am going through with _____

I can go through with _____

Examples of positive prayer:

Supplication:	Please heal me.
Admit:	I believe I'm healed.
Command:	Be healed.
Proclaim:	I'm healed.
Thanksgiving:	Thank you for healing me.

Application and Practice

■ We have studied Fourth Dimensional Spirituality:Words (Application). Share with one another if you have learned anything new.

■ Review "Developing Fourth Dimensional Words" and share with one another about how you can apply this lesson to your lives.

■ Share with each other about how important the power of communication is in your lives.

■ Spend some time in prayer to exercise holy influence on people around you through your positive words (three minutes).

Key Bible Words
The tongue has the power of life and death, and those who love it will eat its fruit (Proverbs 18:21).

Quote
"Words are our thoughts, dressed up and marching on before people. Therefore do not go out wearing filthy clothes."

—Horace

Homework
Make a list of more than five instances in which you complimented and encouraged others.

_____

_____

_____

_____

_____

_____

Bibliography
Life Ends Up with What Is Said by Sato Domio

Whale Done!: The Power of Positive Relationships by Kenneth Blanchard, Thad Lacinak, Chuck Tompkins, and Jim Ballard.

~Notes~

10

LESSON

Developing Fourth Dimensional Spirituality

PRAYER DISCIPLINE

During World War II, France was occupied by German troops for two weeks. Three hundred fifty thousand of England's troops were heavily attacked by Germany on the Deonkeokeu Peninsula, and their fate hung by a thread. King George the IV declared a day of Prayer in England, and the king, cabinet, public officials at their offices, workers at their factories, and farmers in their fileds all prayed in the midst of the war.

As soon as they began to pray, God's answer appeared. While 350,000 English troops on the Deonkeokeu Peninsula were crossing the Dover Channel, a huge storm arose on the German side so that no aircraft could take off and no tank could move. They could not help but look on as the English troops escaped.

On the English side of the Dover Channel the waves were so calm and peaceful that numerous warships were able to help English troops arrive safely in England.

After this, the king and all the people in England held a grand service of thanksgiving unto God.

❖ *When have you experienced the power of prayer?*

The Significance of Self-discipline

Fourth Dimensional Spirituality requires discipline. Through prayer, God's Words, and spiritual training, we can draw closer to God. No matter what type it is, the Christian discipline must be focused on being equipped with God's thought, God's faith, God's dream, and God's Word. Through what process are they instilled in us?

Repeat! Repeat!

By repetition, the Word of God becomes a part of our whole being. There are steps we can take in our life to make sure that the Word of God is absorbed by our entire being—body, soul, and spirit. You will want to implement these vital steps in your life!

The Steps to Make God's Word a Part of You
The steps presented below show the process. Some are acquired and developed in us.

1. Unconsciousness and Unskillfulness

The stage of "unconsciousness and unskillfulness" is a stage in which we do not recognize our own behavior or habits. For instance, there is a stage before we learn how to read, write, play piano, or operate a computer. It is not only a time when we do not realize the *need* to learn new skills, but also a time when we have no interest in learning new skills.

2. Consciousness and Unskillfulness

The stage of "consciousness and unskillfulness" is a stage in which new behavior is recognized, but not yet developed. During this stage, new behavior does not look natural, and in some cases, it is even stressful. However, with good effort, we can move onto the next stage.

3. Consciousness and Skillfulness

The stage of "consciousness and skillfulness" is a stage when we get used to new behavior and a new skill without any trouble. For example, it is like a child who has learned to use the toilet, or someone who can type, or play a musical instrument.

4. Unconsciousness and Skillfulness

The stage of "unconsciousness and skillfulness" is a stage when we are no more conscious performing a certain behavior or skill—activities such as brushing your teeth or using the toilet; everything is done so naturally. In this stage, an alcoholic gets drunk unconsciously.

❖ *In what aspect of your Christian life do you want to achieve the last and fourth stage of unconsciousness and ukillfulness?*

Encounter with the Bible

Please Read Ephesians 6:18-24:

And pray in the Spirit on all occasions with all kinds of prayers and requests. With this in mind, be alert and always keep on praying for all the saints. Pray also for me, that whenever I open my mouth, words may be given me so that I will fearlessly make known the mystery of the gospel, for which I am an ambassador in chains. Pray that I may declare it fearlessly, as I should. Tychicus, the dear brother and faithful servant in the Lord, will tell you everything, so that you also may know how I am and what I am doing. I am sending him to you for this very purpose, that you may know how we are, and that he may encourage you. Peace to the brothers, and love with faith from God the Father and the Lord Jesus Christ. Grace to all who love our Lord Jesus Christ with an undying love.

1. The Scripture text is a letter that Paul sent to the saints in Ephesus, explaining how to be victorious in spiritual warfare. What does Paul tell them to pray? (v.18)

   _____

   _____

2. Believers should pray without ceasing, and in whom does Paul advise them to pray? (v.18)

   _____

   _____

3. Paul asked them to pray for all saints and for him. What is the prayer request that Paul asked them to pray for him about? (v.19)

   _____

   _____

4. Prayer is a divine power to demolish the strongholds of Satan and strength to open the gate to preach the Gospel. Share with one another if you have experienced the door for the Gospel being opened through your prayer.

   _____

   _____

5. What God wants for us is grace in Jesus Christ (v.23, 24). Share with one another regarding your understanding about the relationship between prayer and the grace of Jesus Christ.

Kinds of Prayer that Can Develop Fourth Dimensional Prayer Discipline

Prayer holds an important part in our lives. Because prayer is the breathing of the Spirit, our spirit cannot live if we do not we pray. Fourth Dimensional Spirituality can be cultivated more and more through prayer.

1. Scriptural Prayer

Scriptural prayer is to pray using Scripture or meditating on it. It leads us to pray the right words, and it gives power to our prayers. The best way to pray is with the love of God's Word.

Scriptural Example:

And this is my prayer: that your love may abound more and more in knowledge and depth of insight, so that you may be able to discern what is best and may be pure and blameless until the day of Christ, filled with the fruit of righteousness that comes through Jesus Christ—to the glory and praise of God (Philippians 1:9-11).

Exercise:
Pray the prayer above, putting *your* name in place of the word "your."

Scriptural Example:
The God of our Lord Jesus Christ, the glorious Father, may give you the Spirit of wisdom and revelation, so that you may know him better. I pray also that the eyes of your heart may be enlightened in order that you may know the hope to which he has called you, the riches of his glorious inheritance in the saints, and his incomparably great power for us who believe (Ephesians 1:17-19).

Exercise:
Put the names of people you're praying for in place of "you" and pray for them.

2. Speaking in Tongues

Speaking in tongues is praying with the language God has given you. It is the spiritual language of God's kingdom in which the Holy Spirit speaks through us. By speaking in tongues, we can enter the profound world of prayer.

❖ *Talk to each other about how we can receive the gift of speaking in tongues, and also how we can activate it.*

3. Image Prayer

Image prayer is to pray by envisioning in faith, an image of a person or a fact. While meditation puts focus on conversation with God through meditating on God's Word, image prayer is a prayer picturing a certain situation to put yourself in and inviting Jesus there.

Example:
There is a man who is sick. You want to pray for him. Now, imagine the sick man. He is lying on a bed with pain. Invite Jesus beside him. Jesus is standing by him. You say to Jesus, "Lord, look at him. What a pity he is! Unless you heal him, he has no way of getting well. Please lay your hands on him, Lord." Now, imagine Jesus spreading out His arms to put His hands on the man. He holds the man by the hand, saying, "My beloved, poor son (daughter), I heal you. Be healed and be healthy from now." Right at that moment, he is healed and throws himself in Jesus's arms.

You can apply image prayer to any prayer request. It is not an arbitrary imagination. Rather it is a prayer applying the "power of looking forward" in faith in the spiritual world. Try praying an image prayer.

4. Tabernacle-type Prayer

Tabernacle-type Prayer is to pray following the pattern of the tabernacle of the Old Testament. It is to pray starting from the Altar of Burnt Offering in the Courtyard, to the Basin for Washing, then entering the Holy Place at the Lampstand, the Table, the Altar of Incense, and to the Ark in the Most Holy Place and the throne of God.

Example:

- At the Altar of Burnt Offering: Give thanks to God who delivered us from sin, death, and curse, through the blood of Jesus.

- At the Basin for Washing: Repent to cleanse your soul from sin with water.

- At the Lampstand: Invite the light of the Spirit into your heart.

- At the Table: Repent of your sins, and of not living according to God's Word. Also, ask to make you a man or woman of God's word.

- At the Altar of Incense: Give Him my praise, thanksgiving, and worship.

- At the Ark: Praise the Lord, who is the New Covenant before the Ark, which represents the presence of God.

- At the throne of God: open your heart and pray to God.

There are various other kinds of prayers that will also help you gain discipline in Fourth Dimensional Spirituality, such as the Blood of Jesus prayer and the Lord's prayer.

Application and Practice

■ We have studied "Developing Fourth Dimensional Spirituality: Prayer Discipline." Share with one another if you have learned anything new.

■ A prayer diary is a record of requests and answers of prayer. Try writing a prayer diary for one week.

■ Discuss together and introduce any model of prayer you often practice in addition to the ones you have just learned.

■ Have a time of prayer, asking God to make your life filled with the power of prayer (three minutes).

Key Bible Words
"Pray also for me, that whenever I open my mouth, words may be given me so that I will fearlessly make known the mystery of the gospel" (Proverbs 29:18).

Quote
"Far more things the world dreams of are carried out by prayers."

— Tennyson

Homework

Select ten Bible verses and pray scriptural prayers with them.

Bibliography

Prayer Revival Project by Dr. Joshua Young Gi Hong

~Notes~

Developing Fourth Dimensional Spirituality

WORD DISCIPLINE

This is a true story: A pastor was imprisoned on a charge of initiating anti-state prayer meetings under the regime of president Park Jung Hee. He was put in solitary confinement and was tormented by severe cold. The pastor prayed, "Lord, this is more than I can bear. Help me please." He opened the Bible and started to read passages regarding fires. The first one he found was in Exodus chapter 3 when Moses saw the burning bush at Mount Horeb. Next he read how Isaiah was touched by a live coal from the altar in Isaiah chapter 6. Then he read how Elijah competed with 450 prophets of Baal by fire.

In the New Testament, he read Luke 12:49 where Jesus said He came to bring fire on earth. Then he reached the first part of Acts chapter 2, where the fire of the Holy Spirit came on the day of Pentecost. While he was reading verses 3 and 4, he started to feel a certain change in his body. Without his knowing how it was happening, he became warm and was not cold anymore. He touched the floor, and it was warm. Then he put his hands on the walls, and they were also warm, as if a steam heater was working.

The pastor acknowledged it was a fire of the Holy Spirit answering his prayer. At that very moment joy overflowed from his heart, and in tears he gave thanks to God. Previously, he had suffered from frostbite, but that night when he experienced the fire of the Holy Spirit, he found himself cured completely of it. Since then, every year at this time, he fasts, remembering the blessings he had received. His name is Pastor Jin Hong Kim of Durae Church.

❖ *Share with one another regarding what is necessary in order to experience the power of God's Word?*

The "Glasses" for Meditation on the Scripture

In order to meditate on the Scripture effectively, we need a tool for it. The reason we fail in meditating on the Scripture is because we look at the texts without wearing "spiritual glasses." Presented below are the *glasses* that are necessary when you read the Bible:

1. Who is God (Jesus, the Holy Spirit)?

2. What sin I should stop committing?

3. What is the promise I should hold on to?

4. What is the commandment I should obey?

5. What is the falsehood I should avoid?

6. What is the example I should follow?

7. What is the truth I have found out anew?

Scriptural Example:

> *Peace I leave with you; my peace I give you. I do not give to you as the world gives. Do not let your hearts be troubled and do not be afraid. You heard me say, I am going away and I am coming back to you. If you loved me, you would be glad that I am going to the Father, for the Father is greater than I (John 14:27-28).*

The Glasses for Meditating on the Scripture: Answers

Below I have listed some possible examples of the answers to the questions above:

1. *Who is God (Jesus)?*
   He is God, who gives me peace and always comes back to me.

2. *What is sin I should stop committing?*
   The sin of not having peace, but being worried.

3. *What is the commandment I should obey?*
   Not to be troubled and afraid.

❖ *Choose a text, and train yourself to wear the "glasses" for meditation.*

Encounter with the Bible

Read Hebrew 4:11-16:

> *Let us, therefore, make every effort to enter that rest, so that no one will fall by following their example of disobedience. For the word of God is living and active. Sharper than any double-edged sword, it penetrates even to dividing soul and spirit, joints and marrow; it judges the thinking and attitudes of the heart. Nothing in all creation is hidden from God's sight. Everything is uncovered and laid bare before the eyes of him to whom we must give account. Therefore, since we have a great high priest who has gone through the heavens, Jesus the Son of God, let us hold firmly to the faith we profess. For we do not have a high*

priest who is unable to sympathize with our weaknesses, but we have one who has been tempted in every way, just as we are—yet was without sin. ¹⁶Let us then approach the throne of grace with confidence, so that we may receive mercy and find grace to help us in our time of need.

1. The Scripture text is a letter of encouragement sent to the ones among Jews who had received Jesus Christ as their Savior. What does the text indirectly say for the Christians to do in order to enter into that rest? (v.11)

_____

_____

_____

2. The object of our obedience is the word of God. What kind of characteristics and power does the Word of God have? (v.12)

    a.

    b.

    c.

3. What is Jesus—by whom the Word of God was incarnated—to us? (v.14)

_____

_____

_____

We can approach the throne of grace through Jesus. Share with each other if you have ever experienced entering the throne of grace through God's Word.

The Scripture is a guide book for our faith. We should have a deep knowledge of the Bible. Christians have to avoid all ideas and actions which deviate from the Scripture. For developing the Fourth Dimensional Spirituality Word Discipline, discipline in reading the Word of God, is a required process.

Our Attitude Toward the Scriptures

1. Remember the purpose of the Bible.

You have to keep in your mind why the Bible was written and what kind of purpose it has. The Scripture is not a textbook holding an ethical message. Instead, it is a book containing a message of salvation (2 Timothy 3:15). Therefore, you should approach the Word of God with a heart searching for the way of salvation.

2. Ask for inspiration of the Holy Spirit.

All Scripture is God-breathed (2 Timothy 3:16, 2 Peter 1:21). Therefore, we have to depend on the Holy Spirit to interpret it instead of human reason or rationality. Call on Him always for help.

3. Try to find a message from the Scripture, rather than just reading it.

It is important to *not only read* the Scriptures, we should find the message for us within them. The Bible is a love letter containing Jesus' love story for us. We should search for His love just as we would search for a treasure.

❖ *Whom should we fix our focus upon when we read the Bible (John 5:39)?*

The Five Models of Word Discipline

There are five models of Word Discipline for developing Fourth Dimensional Spirituality. Consider them and learn to implement them to develop your knowledge of God's Word.

1. Meditate on the Scripture

Meditating on the Word of God is the most basic training. It gives us strength for our daily lives and also promises the victory of Christian living. It is important to constantly meditate on the Word of God everyday.

❖ *How was Joshua able to conquer Canaan (Joshua 1:8)?*

_____

_____

_____

2. Memorize the Scriptures

Memorizing the Scripture transforms our soul dramatically, from the inside out. Memorized Scripture can be of good use when you speak to others (Proverbs 15:23), when you resist Satan (Matthew 4:1-11), and when you hold on to the promise of God in prayer (Ephesians 1:16-17).

3. Research the Scriptures

Scripture is an object for research. If you study the Bible constantly, you can draw deep meaning from it. Remember, the Bible is like a treasure house full of truth.

❖ *What was the characteristic that the Thessalonians had, that allowed them to receive Paul's message in Acts 17:11?*

4. Read the Scriptures

If you want to develop Fourth Dimensional Spirituality, you must read the Scriptures constantly. The more frequently you read through Bible, the deeper you can understand it and eventually, you can experience great victory in Christian living.

5. Hear the Scriptures

The Bible is called the "the written Word" of God. However, before the written Word, there was "the spoken Word" which was given to the writers of the Bible. We can hear the *voice of God* speaking to us through the written Word. It is the highest stage of Bible reading.

Below is a passage written by Michael Mitton, who is the author of *Still Small Voice*. Read it, and try to apply it to your life:

> *"It is good to be ready to receive God's voice at any time of the day. However, it is necessary to set a time regularly to hear His voice. To hear Him consistently, you'd better choose a time that is set apart for the Lord so that you will not be interrupted by anything but God."*

Application and Practice

■ We have studied developing Fourth Dimensional Spirituality: Word Discipline. Share with one another if you have learned anything new.

■ Share with one another about which, among the Five Models of Word Discipline, is most necessary to develop Fourth Dimensional Spirituality.

■ Share with one another if you have ever experienced any obstacles to spending time meditating on the Scripture.

■ Have a time of prayer asking God to make your life full of His Word (three minutes).

Key Bible Words

For the word of God is living and active. Sharper than any double-edged sword, it penetrates even to dividing soul and spirit, joints and marrow; it judges the thinking and attitudes of the heart (Hebrews 4:12).

Quote

"Early in the morning, I started to meditate on what blessing I can find in the Scripture. Then my soul came to a place where I can have real communication with God."

—George Muller

Homework

Meditate on the Scripture and write an essay sharing your thinking.

Bibliography

Guide School for the Bible by Dr. David Yonggi Cho

~Notes~

12

LESSON

Developing Fourth Dimensional Spirituality

THE HOLY SPIRIT DISCIPLINE

John Bunyan, an Englishman, produced the Puritans and was imprisoned on a charge of violating the edict of the king. One day a chief guard secretly opened the prison door for his superior and allowed Bunyan to have a short visit with his family. On his way back to the prison, John Bunyan said, "Thanks for your favor, but I had to come back because the Holy Spirit did not allow me...." One hour later, the king made an official visit to the prison. The king then went back after he made sure that Bunyan was still there. The chief guard told Bunyan, "Because you have acted according to the Holy Spirit, you could be safe and so could I."

❖ *Have you ever experienced avoiding trouble or failure by following the guidance of the Holy Spirit?*

Men Who Walked in the Holy Spirit

It is a valuable lesson to catch a glimpse of the way men of God have lived in times gone by. In this lesson, I have listed several, along with their inspiring stories.

John Wesley

"On the morning of May 24, 1738, I was reading the commentary of Romans. At about 9:15, strangely enough, I experienced a warm feeling in my heart. I had noticed I was in Christ and was filled with the joy that comes from the Lord dwelling in my heart, the same heart where all lustful desires and sins come from."

John Wesley could not refrain from his joy, and he came out to spread the Good News. The ministry of the Holy Spirit spread so greatly that it led to the beginning of Methodism, which eventually saved England, a country on the brink of collapse due to its depravity and corruption.

Charles Finney

Charles Finney was a key figure of the second Great Awakening in the United States in the nineteenth century. It is said that people repented with tears when he stared at them with his big

71

eyes. When he preached, various physical phenomena followed, such as rolling, running, crying, and shaking. These phenomena became present after he experienced the Holy Spirit: *It was like an electric wave penetrating his spirit and his body.* After this spiritual experience, he was able to carry out his ministry with the power and conviction of his calling.

D. L. Moody

One day, Dwight Moody, thirty-four years of age, was walking down a street in New York. He cried out, "Oh Lord, why do you not let me walk with you everyday? Save me from my wretchedness. Hold me strong and anoint me with your Spirit, please."

All of a sudden, the power of the Spirit convicted him to come to his friend's house which was nearby. He asked his friend for a room where he could stay alone, and he started to pray in a strange language, something he had never experienced before. Afterwards, the power of his ministry doubled.

Charles Spurgeon

The preacher Charles Spurgeon said to the students in his class, "We need the Holy Spirit working with us in order to bear fruit in our ministries. To speak six words with the power of the Holy Spirit is better than to preach for sixty years without the Holy Spirit."

It is said when Charles Spurgeon went up to the pulpit before he preached, he repeated to himself, "I believe in the Holy Spirit; I trust in Him." Thus, it is most important to have an attitude that personally invites the Holy Spirit and trusts in Him.

❖ *Find out anything you have in common with these powerful men and share it with one another.*

Encounter with the Bible

Please Read Galatians 5: 16-23:
So I say, live by the Spirit, and you will not gratify the desires of the sinful nature. For the sinful nature desires what is contrary to the Spirit, and the Spirit what is contrary to the sinful nature. They are in conflict with each other, so that you do not do what you want. But if you are led by the Spirit, you are not under law. The acts of the sinful nature are obvious: sexual immorality, impurity and debauchery; idolatry and witchcraft; hatred, discord, jealousy, fits of rage, selfish ambition, dissensions, factions and envy; drunkenness, orgies, and the like. I warn you, as I did before, that those who live like this will not inherit the kingdom of God. But the fruit of the Spirit is love, joy, peace, patience, kindness, goodness, faithfulness, gentleness and self-control. Against such things there is no law.

1. The Scripture text is about the ministry of the Holy Spirit, which the Apostle Paul talks about in the midst of also talking about the freedom of being a Christian. Christians receive freedom in the Lord, but they are not exempt from conflicts in life. What does the text say our conflict is laid between? (v.16)

2. What can we avoid if we live by the Spirit? (v.18-21)

_____

_____

_____

3. What is the final destiny for those who gratify the desires of sinful nature? (v.21)

_____

4. Make a list of the nine fruits of the Spirit and share the meanings of each of them. (v.22-23)

Fruit of the Spirit	Meaning
1. _____	_____
2. _____	_____
3. _____	_____
4. _____	_____
5. _____	_____
6. _____	_____
7. _____	_____
8. _____	_____
9. _____	_____

In the Scripture text, there is a contrast between fifteen acts of the sinful nature and the nine fruits of the Spirit. It is required to make an effort not to sin, but it is better to be filled with the Holy Spirit and bear the fruits of the Spirit. Have you ever experienced being driven to despair by the power of the sin working within you and realized the need to be filled with the Spirit and earnestly asked for it?

_____

_____

The Holy Spirit is a gift and a source of life that is given to all Christians. *The Holy Spirit is God, a Person and Advocate.* When Christians believe in Jesus, they will receive the gift of the Holy Spirit and the blessing of walking with Him.

Steps to Accomplish Holy Spirit Discipline for Fourth Dimensional Spirituality
The helpful steps below are the method whereby you can develop Fourth Dimension Spirituality:

1. Admit the initiative of the Holy Spirit.

The Holy Spirit is not static, having no movement. Rather, He is the Spirit that is leading our entire life. The Holy Spirit directed the Israelites (Isaiah 63:11) and so He does with the lives of today's Christians.

2. Understand the extensive ministry of the Holy Spirit.

The Holy Spirit is not possessed exclusively by a certain denomination or system. The Holy Spirit ministers more broadly than we can imagine. His ministry is endless, which includes taking part in creation, making people born again, comforting the church, and so on.

❖ *In Particular, the ministry of the Holy Spirit can be extended to purifying society. Search for cases in church history, in which revival in the Spirit was linked to social purification movements.*

3. Be anointed with the Holy Spirit.

Anointing is the presence of God. Jesus became the Messiah when He was anointed. We also can do Messianic ministry when we are anointed as Jesus (Luke 4:18). In other words, we not only perceive the truth, but we can pass it on to others.

❖ *What kind of power did Apolos experience when he, who used to know the Word of God only on an intellectual level, was filled with the Holy Spirit (Acts 19:6)?*

4. Walk in the Holy Spirit personally.

It is so important to understand the Holy Spirit as a personal God. If we understand the Holy Spirit only as a strength or power, we may be in danger of trying to *use* Him as a tool rather than being immersed by Him (Acts 8:19).

5. Work with the Holy Spirit and be united with Him.

The Holy Spirit is like an older colleague. We should earnestly ask the Holy Spirit to work with us in everything. In particular, we should desire spiritual gifts so that, through the power and strength the Holy Spirit gives us, we can do God's work. Then we can have perfect unity with Him.

❖ *Talk to one another about how we can set our minds on what the Spirit desires(Romans 8:5).*

The Definition of the Advocate
The Holy Spirit is scripturally defined by the characteristics below:
1. Helper
2. Comforter
3. Teacher
4. Teller
5. Counselor

Fourth Dimensional Spirituality and Spiritual Authority

The Discipline of Prayer, of words, and of the Holy Spirit, arms us with God's thought, faith, dream, and words. The armament of the Fourth Dimensional Spirituality lets us realize the spiritual authority and teaches us to make use of it. It is so important to utilize spiritual authority for spiritual victory in the Christian life and for the revival of the Church.

May you all experience the creative transformation through Fourth Dimensional Spirituality, so that you can become miracle-makers.

Application and Practice

■ We have studied Developing Fourth Dimensional Spirituality: The Holy Spirit Discipline. Share with one another if you have learned anything new.

■ Share with one another about the meaning of "the fullness and the anointing of the Holy Spirit."

■ Share with one another about what is the most important prerequisite to being a "spiritual person."

■ Have a time of prayer that God would enable you to have a life full of the power of the Holy Spirit (three minutes).

Key Bible Words
So I say, live by the Spirit, and you will not gratify the desires of the sinful nature (Galatians 5:16).

Quote
"When people surrender themselves to the Holy Spirit, they learn more about God, Jesus Christ and salvation in a week than they learn for a lifetime apart from the Holy Spirit."
—John Brown

Homework
In all things, rely on the Holy Spirit and take time to have communication with Him.

Bibliography
The Holy Spirit School by Dr. David Yonggi Cho

~Notes~

Fourth Dimension Spirituality: Answers

ANSWERS TO THE STUDY QUESTIONS

Lesson 1

1. Being sure of what we hope for and certain of what we do not see.
2. God's command.
3. Faith.
4. To believe that He exists and that He rewards those who earnestly seek Him.

Lesson 2

1. What nature desires versus what the Spirit desires.
2. Death versus life and peace.
3. The sinful mind is hostile to God. It does not submit to God's law, nor can it do so.
4. Having the Spirit of Christ.

Lesson 3

1. To stay [abide] in the Lord always.
2. To present requests to God by prayer and petition, with thanksgiving.
3. The peace of God which transcends all understanding.
4. Whatever is true, whatever is noble, whatever is right, whatever is pure, whatever is lovely, whatever is admirable.

Lesson 4

1. God is He who gives life to the dead and calls things that are not as though they were.
2. Against all hope, Abraham in hope believed.
3. The promise of God.
4. Being fully persuaded that God had power to do what He had promised.

Lesson 5

1. Threw him into fire or water to kill him.
2. Unbelieving.
3. To come out of him and never enter him again.
4. Prayer.

Lesson 6

1. Be ashamed.
2. His Spirit (The Holy Spirit).
3. a) Sons and daughters: prophesy.
   b) Young men: dream dreams.
   c) Old men: see visions.
4. Everyone who calls on the name of the LORD

Lesson 7

1. To lift up eyes and look north and south, east, and west.
2. a) All the land that he sees God will give to him and his offspring.
   b) God will make his offspring like the dust of the earth.
3. He built an altar to the LORD.

Lesson 8

1. When God permits him.
2. To curse God and die.
3. God.
4. By confession with our mouths.

Lesson 9

1. He let them turn back and set out toward the desert along the route to the Red Sea.
2. The complaints against God.
3. Their bodies will fall in the desert.
4. Following God wholeheartedly.

Lesson 10

1. On all occasions.
2. In the Spirit.
3. To open his mouth, that words may be given him so that he will fearlessly make known the mystery of the Gospel.

Lesson 11

1. Have faith.
2. a. The Word of God is living and active.
   b. It's sharper than any double-edged sword, it penetrates even to dividing soul and spirit, joints and marrow.
   c. It judges the thinking and attitudes of the heart.
3. A great High Priest.

1. Never let this Book of the Law depart from his mouth; meditate on it day and night, so that he may be careful to do everything written in it.
3. They received the message with great eagerness and examined the Scriptures every day.

Lesson 12

1. The Spirit and the desires of the sinful nature.
2. Sexual immorality, impurity, and debauchery; idolatry and witchcraft; hatred, discord, jealousy, fits of rage, selfish ambition, dissensions, factions and envy; drunkenness, orgies.
3. They will not inherit the kingdom of God.
4. Love, joy, peace, patience, kindness, goodness, faithfulness, gentleness, and self-control.

3. He spoke in tongues and prophesied.

~Notes~